A Picture Book of
Eleanor Roosevelt

In memory of my sister-in-law Felice,
1944-1989,
who had the generous spirit of
Eleanor Roosevelt in her.

D.A.A.

Text copyright © 1991 by David A. Adler
Illustrations copyright © 1991 by Robert Casilla
All rights reserved
Printed in the United States of America

Library of Congress Cataloging-in-Publication Data

Adler, David A.
A picture book of Eleanor Roosevelt / by David A. Adler;
illustrated by Robert Casilla.—1st ed.
p.   cm.
Summary: A brief account of the life and
accomplishments of Eleanor Roosevelt.
ISBN 0-8234-0856-6
1. Roosevelt, Eleanor, 1884-1962—Pictorial works—
Juvenile literature. 2. Presidents—United States—Wives—
Pictorial works—Juvenile literature.   [1. Roosevelt, Eleanor, 1884-1962.
2. First ladies.]   I. Casilla, Robert, ill.   II.Title.
E807.1.R48A66   1991
973.917'092—dc20
[B]
[92]   90-39212   CIP   AC
ISBN 0-8234-1157-5 (pbk.)

A Picture Book of
Eleanor Roosevelt

David A. Adler

illustrated by Robert Casilla

Holiday House / New York

Eleanor Roosevelt was born in New York City on October 11, 1884. Her parents, Anna and Elliot, were wealthy. They had many servants, a home in the city, and a large summer house in the country.

Eleanor's mother was beautiful, but Eleanor was not a pretty child. She was tall and awkward and also very quiet. She often looked so serious that her mother called her "Granny." Eleanor hated that nickname.

Eleanor's father called her his "Little Golden Hair" and his "Little Nell." Eleanor loved those names and she loved her father.

When Eleanor was just eight years old, her mother died. Eleanor went to live in her grandmother's house. Two years later, in 1894, Eleanor's father died, too. Eleanor missed him terribly and dreamed of him often.

There were many rules in her grandmother's house. Eleanor could not read in bed before breakfast. She had to wear long black stockings and high button shoes even in the summer.

Eleanor was cared for by a servant, Madeleine, who often screamed at her. Sometimes she even pulled Eleanor's hair.

When Eleanor was fifteen, she was sent to Allenswood, a boarding school in England. She was happy to go. She felt she was starting a new life.

The teachers and students at Allenswood thought Eleanor was wonderful. The headmistress wrote home that Eleanor had a pure heart. She taught Eleanor the importance of helping others.

While Eleanor was in England, her uncle, Theodore Roosevelt, became the president of the United States. He was a strong and popular leader.

Eleanor returned to New York in 1902. She was almost eighteen years old.

Eleanor's grandmother sent her from one fancy party to the next. Eleanor usually hated those parties, but she did have a good time when she talked with her distant cousin, Franklin Delano Roosevelt.

Eleanor joined the Junior League and began a lifelong devotion to helping the poor. While working for the Junior League, Eleanor taught children to dance and exercise, in the Rivington Street Settlement House.

Eleanor took her cousin Franklin to the Settlement House. Franklin took her to college football games at his school. They fell in love.

On March 17, 1905 Eleanor and Franklin were married. At the wedding, the guests paid little attention to the bride and groom. They were more interested in Eleanor's uncle, President Theodore Roosevelt.

Eleanor and Franklin had six children—one daughter and five sons. One son died when he was still an infant. Eleanor had servants and nurses to help her. At times, the children were afraid of the strict nurses and so was Eleanor.

Franklin's mother Sara often told Franklin and Eleanor what to do. Sara chose their first house and furniture. During the early years of her marriage, Eleanor didn't complain, but later she refused to be bossed around.

Franklin admired Eleanor's uncle Theodore and wanted to be just like him. Eleanor helped Franklin campaign for public office.

In 1921 Franklin was stricken with polio. He couldn't walk after that. When Franklin first became sick, Eleanor was his nurse. Later she went to political meetings and traveled for him. She brought back detailed reports on what she heard and saw.

Franklin was elected governor of New York in 1928 and 1930 and president of the United States in 1932. He was reelected president in 1936, 1940, and 1944. When Franklin became president, Eleanor became first lady.

The 1930s was the time of the Great Depression. Banks and factories had closed. Millions of people had lost their jobs. Hungry people stood in long lines for free bread and soup. It was a difficult time to be president or first lady.

Eleanor didn't wait to do things. Her motto was, "To-morrow is now." She had a radio program and wrote a daily newspaper column. She traveled to cities, towns, farms and into coal mines. She brought hope to millions of people.

Eleanor used the money she earned from her speeches and writings to help the poor.

Eleanor spoke out for women's rights, the rights of Indians, the homeless, young people, and minorities. She told people, "Do what you feel in your heart to be right." Eleanor always did.

Eleanor belonged to the Daughters of the American Revolution. In 1939 they would not allow a great singer, Marian Anderson, to perform in their hall because she was black. Eleanor quit the group and arranged for Marian Anderson to sing in front of the Lincoln Memorial instead.

On December 7, 1941 the United States' armed forces were attacked at Pearl Harbor, Hawaii. The United States entered the Second World War.

During the war, Eleanor traveled all over the world to visit American soldiers. When she came home, she brought messages from the soldiers to their families.

On April 12, 1945 President Franklin Roosevelt died.
The whole country mourned with Eleanor.

Eleanor moved out of the White House. She was no
longer the first lady, but she did not retire from public
life. "Life was meant to be lived," she said.

The war ended a few months later, and Eleanor worked to ensure peace. She was the United States' representative at the new United Nations, where leaders from all over the world could meet and discuss their differences. Eleanor said, "If we are to live together, we have to talk."

While Eleanor was at the United Nations, she was the chairperson of the Commission on Human Rights.

Eleanor was always busy. "You must do the thing you think you cannot do," she said.

Eleanor Roosevelt died on November 7, 1962. She was the most important, most loved woman of her time. President Harry S. Truman called her "First Lady of the World."

IMPORTANT DATES

1884	Born on October 11 in New York City.
1905	Married Franklin Delano Roosevelt on March 17.
1921	Franklin was stricken with polio.
1928–1932	Franklin served as governor of New York.
1932–1945	Franklin served as president and Eleanor as first lady of the United States.
1945	Franklin died on April 12.
1945–1953	Eleanor served as a delegate to the United Nations.
1946–1951	Served as chairperson of the United Nations Human Rights Commission.
1962	Died on November 7 at the age of 78.